OCS Report
MMS 2010-025

Investigation of Fatality
Green Canyon Block 304, Well No. 1
OCS-G 28066
3 September 2009

Gulf of Mexico
Off the Louisiana Coast

U.S. Department of the Interior
Minerals Management Service
Gulf of Mexico OCS Regional Office

New Orleans
February 2010

OCS Report
MMS 2010-025

Investigation of Fatality
Green Canyon Block 304, Well No. 1
OCS-G 28066
3 September 2009

Gulf of Mexico
Off the Louisiana Coast

Glynn T. Breaux – Chair
Ben Coco
Josh Ladner
Jason Mathews

U.S. Department of the Interior
Minerals Management Service
Gulf of Mexico OCS Regional Office

New Orleans
February 2010

Contents

Recommendations 41

List of Figures

List of Tables

Abbreviations and Acronyms

ACO	Acting Crane Operator
ADF	Acting Deck Foreman
ATP	Acting Tool Pusher
DP	Deck Pusher
FOCUS	Formulate, Organize, Communicate, Undertake and Summarize
HSE	Health, Safety & Environmental
HSPP	Health and Safety Policies and Procedures Manual
IP	Injured Person
MMS	Minerals Management Service
MOC	Management of Change
OCS	Outer Continental Shelf
OIM	Offshore Installation Manager
OSM	MMS Regional Office of Safety Management
Painter/Witness	(Subcontract Painter/Blaster that witnessed accident)
Repsol	(Repsol E&P USA Inc.)
RHSER	Repsol HSE Representative
RSCR	Repsol Senior Company Representative
Rstb 1	Roustabout 1
Rstb 3	Roustabout 3
SEDCO	Southeast Drilling Company
SMART	Specific, Measurable, Achievable, Realistic & Timely
SPPD	Transocean Safety Policies, Procedures and Documentation Risk Management THINK Planning Process
START	See, Think, Act, Reinforce, Track
TRIT	Transocean-Repsol Investigative Team

Executive Summary

An accident that resulted in one fatality occurred on the Transocean *Cajun Express* semi-submersible rig contracted by Repsol E&P USA Inc. (Repsol) to conduct plug and abandonment operations from Lease OCS-G 28066, Green Canyon Block 304, Well No. 1, in the Gulf of Mexico offshore Louisiana, on 3 September 2009 at approximately 1025 hours.

The pipe handler machine was being used to relocate tubulars from the catwalk to the pipe bay deck. A Roustabout was serving as the pipe handler operator (Operator) and supervisor for the task, while being accompanied by another Roustabout acting as a pipe handler spotter (Spotter).

The Operator proceeded to traverse the pipe handler approximately 16 feet on its trolley back to the starboard side in preparation to pick-up the next joint. The Operator then noticed the Spotter was injured and lying down on the pipe deck, so the Operator immediately pressed the pipe handler's emergency stop button. A crush point that existed between the pipe handler's lower travel assembly and one of the trolley's vertical support stanchions had pinned and crushed the head of the Spotter. The Spotter suffered severe head trauma and was first attended to by the onsite Medic who found no signs of life. The Spotter was later pronounced deceased at the accident scene by the attending Medi-vac personnel.

The Minerals Management Service (MMS) accident investigation Panel concluded that the **Cause** of the accident was: 1) the pipe handler Operator's failure to confirm an "all clear" or a "Time Out for Safety" (Stop Work authority) when the Spotter was out-of-sight. **Contributing Causes** include Transocean line management's failure to: 1) provide a more formalized training program to include the hazards associated with the pipe handler, 2) identify the specific pipe handler operational tasks, hazards and respective mitigations in order to develop and implement guidelines for personnel working around the strong-back area, 3) provide additional onsite supervision to both the Operator and Spotter during the pipe handler operation and 4) properly implement their Management of Change policy. **A Possible Contributing Causes** was: 1) the work area involved a hot work environment in direct sunlight.

Introduction

Authority

A fatal accident occurred on 3 September 2009 at approximately 1025 hours aboard the Transocean *Cajun Express* semi-submersible rig contracted to Repsol E&P USA Inc. (Repsol), while plug and abandonment operations were being conducted on Lease OCS-G 28066, Green Canyon Block 304 Well No. 1, in the Gulf of Mexico offshore Louisiana. Pursuant to 43 U.S.C. 1348(d)(1) and (2) and (f) [Outer Continental Shelf (OCS) Lands Act, as amended] and Department of the Interior regulations 30 CFR 250, the Minerals Management Service (MMS) is required to investigate and prepare a report of this accident. By memorandum dated 16 September 2009, the following personnel were named to the investigative panel:

Glynn T. Breaux, Chairman – Office of Safety Management, Field Operations, GOM OCS Region
Ben Coco – Houma District, Field Operations, GOM OCS Region
Josh Ladner – Houma District, Field Operations, GOM OCS Region
Jason Mathews – Accident Investigation Board, Office of Offshore Regulatory Programs

Background

Lease OCS-G 28066 covers approximately 5,760 acres and is located in Green Canyon Block 304, Gulf of Mexico, off the Louisiana Coast (*see Figure 1*). The lease was purchased in Sale Number 198 by three owners, with an effective lease date of 1 July 2006, and an expiration date of 30 June 2016. Repsol USA Inc. is the record title interest owner effective 1 June 2006, and was designated operator on 13 November 2008, by Chevron USA Inc. with Chevron USA Inc. and Repsol USA Inc. each holding 50% interest.

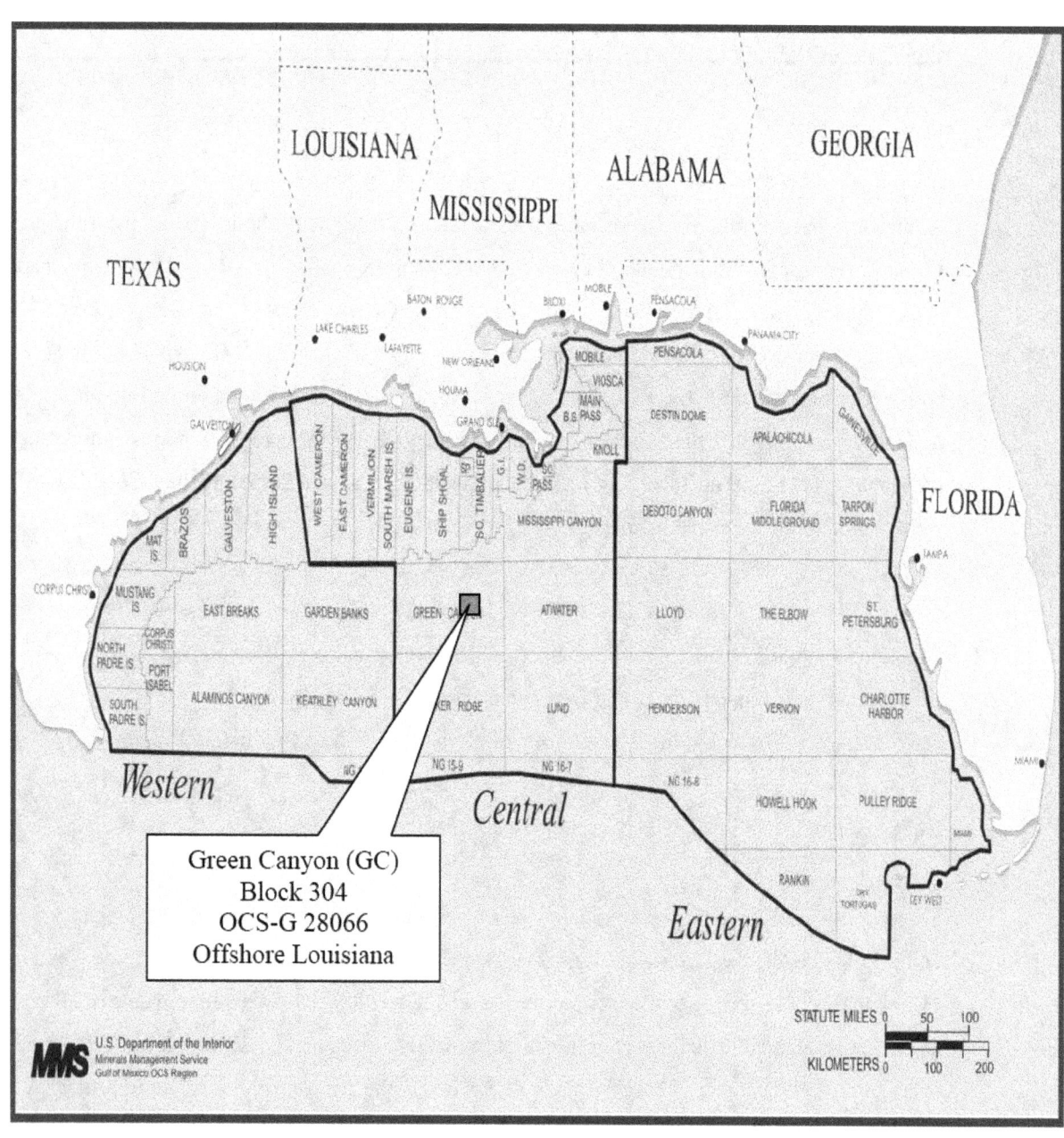

Figure 1: Location of Lease OCS-G 28066, Green Canyon Block 304, Offshore Louisiana

4

Findings

Preliminary Data

    Short Change Crew

It's important to be aware that a short change crew was in place. The short change crew involved multiple employees filling new roles and/or not working on their normal crew shift during the time of the accident. The regular Tool Pusher, Deck Foreman and Assistant Crane Operator were all on personal leave, and a Roustabout had passed away on his time off. This created a need to change positions and bring personnel from another crew. A Roustabout with a Class B Operator's certificate was designated the Acting Crane Operator and task supervisor to manage multiple rig tasks with a newly created and relatively inexperienced crew without additional Transocean management oversight. A Roustabout was acting as the pipe handler Operator and supervisor of the operation, with a Roustabout that normally served as a Floorhand acting in the role of the pipe handler Spotter (the deceased).

Pre-Job Safety Meetings and Corresponding Safety Documents

The Transocean THINK Planning Process utilizes the Transocean Written Think Plan, Think Process Checklist and Task Specific Think Procedure Forms to assist in reducing/eliminating operational task risks to as low as reasonably practicable. The Written Think Plan identifies the task steps, equipment and materials needed to be inspected, hazards identification with control measures, responsible personnel, and communication assignments for personnel not part of the plan in order to maintain control. The Think Process Checklist is used to develop the Written Think Plan in order to plan the tasks, inspect the appropriate areas, identify the hazards, and communicate to all in order to control the overall operation. Each task of the Written Think Plan can be further analyzed by use of the Task Specific Think Procedure.

The deck crews held pre-job safety meetings to include the use of four Written Think Plans with corresponding Think Process Checklists that were discussed and signed by the crew members prior to the start of moving the drill pipe from the drill floor in the early morning hours of 3 September 2009. The Written Think Plans with corresponding Think Process

Checklists and Task Specific Think Plan consisted of utilizing the rig's pedestal crane for making lifts to/from the rig floor (attended by both the Operator and Spotter), rearranging deck cargo (attended by the Operator), offloading/back-loading the cargo vessel with a pedestal crane (attended by the Operator), and laying-down drill pipe at the starboard mouse hole using the porch hoist in preparation for the pipe handler operation (attended by the Operator). None of these documents were completed for the actual pipe handling operation of retrieving the pipe from the catwalk and traversing the pipe to set down onto the pipe bay deck. In addition, Transocean Prompt Cards were utilized to ensure that effective Think Plans (written and verbal) are created. The Prompt Cards are essentially a Job Safety Analysis that prompts personnel in evaluating operational tasks, hazards and consequences in order to implement control measures to reduce the risk. However, no Prompt Cards were utilized for the pipe handler operation.

Subsequent to the last Written Think Plan meeting for laying-down pipe at the starboard mouse hole, the Operator and Spotter went down to the pipe bay deck to begin the pipe handler operation of retrieving the pipe from the catwalk and transferring it to the pipe bay deck.

Timeline of Events

According to the Transocean investigation report, the following timeline includes those significant activities the morning of the accident to include preparing the pipe for the pipe handler transfer, and the accident during the pipe handler operation (*see Table 1*).

TABLE 1	
Rig Activities Timeline the day of the Accident	
(derived from the Transocean Investigative Report)	
Date	**Activities**
3 September 2009	
(Hours)	**Night Tour**
(0000 to 0030)	The Deck D Crew completed three (3) Written Think Plans (specific to pedestal crane operations) and a Permit to Work at the crane pedestal. The Operator and Spotter did not participate in these Written Think Plans.
(0215 to 0230)	The Operator and Spotter participated in a Written Think Plan on the rig floor for laying out pipe from the rig floor to the porch hoist V-door; the Written Think Plan was not specific to the pipe handler operation.
(0230 to 0330)	The Operator initiated a verbal Think Plan with the Spotter and the two initiated pipe handler operations (laying out drill collars and the Bottom Hole Assembly) from the catwalk to the pipe bay deck.
(0330 to 0530)	The Operator and Spotter conducted general deck housekeeping.
(0530 to 0600) 0600 0600	The Operator and Spotter took their lunch break. The Deck Pusher began his shift. The Assistant Crane Operator began his shift.
(0600 to 1025)	The Operator and Spotter resumed Pipe Handler operations and continued laying out tubulars from the Porch hoist catwalk to the pipe bay deck for back-loading, while the deck crews continued to back-load the boat.
1025	The accident occurred.

Express Class Pipe Handling Capabilities

Transocean's Sedco Express-class rigs include the Cajun Express, Sedco Express, and Sedco Energy which are all a fifth generation fleet of semi-submersibles that reduce the human interface in drilling operations through the utilization of a mechanized tubular handling processes. These rigs employ concepts for making-up and running drillstring components, riser pipe as well as casing and tubing. Once the riser, drill pipe and casing tubulars are onboard a Sedco Express-class rig, the riser gantry crane, the Pipe Handler tubular transfer system and the Tri-Act Derrick carry out the tubular process with very little direct human involvement. This particular pipe handler system was only manufactured for the three Sedco Express-class rigs, with only the Cajun Express rig working in the Gulf of Mexico at the time of the accident. It should be noted that at the time of publication of this report, none of these rigs are currently working in the Gulf of Mexico.

The porch hoist's V-door/rolling trolley is a pipe and/or riser handling system that allows the tubulars and miscellaneous equipment to be transported in/out of the drill-floor and is remotely controlled from a local operator station or the Driller's cabin. The pipe handler is essentially an overhead gantry crane that travels on a horizontal track, with a pipe racking system to transfer tubulars from the porch hoist/auxiliary rig floor to the rig's pipe deck. The pipe handler utilizes a hoist fitted in a trolley that moves horizontally on a rail. The pipe handler picks up the tubular from the catwalk, near the porch hoist area, where the pipe handler traverses its trolley system to stack the tubulars on the pipe bay deck. Back-loading of the pipe to a cargo vessel then occurs utilizing a pedestal crane.

Pipe Handler Operations/Maintenance Manual for SEDCO – 6 October 2000

Contents of the manual provide a description and operation of the pipe handler, operating instructions, maintenance instructions, a parts list with drawings and data sheets. The pipe handler operates in either the normal mode or maintenance mode, with the maintenance mode only used to lower the pipe or move the pipe handler to a safe position where it can be repaired. The pipe handler is capable of operating at a full travel speed of 118 feet per minute (1.97 feet per second). The manual does not outline a training section, but rather focuses on a pipe handler technical description and operating section. In addition the manual does not identify and isolate the crush point.

Pipe Handler Operator Training/Certification Test

Transocean Operator training for the pipe handler is a two step process. First, a two page study guide is reviewed prior to taking the two page certification test on the rig. The study guide is essentially the certification test with answers that one memorizes in order to complete the sixteen fill-in-the blank, multiple choice, and true-or-false questions. Next, the Operator-in-training observes a qualified Operator performing the pipe handler duties until the Operator-in-training feels confident enough to take the controls while the qualified Operator observes. This entire Operator-in-training to qualified Operator usually takes several hitches. At the time of the accident, the length of a hitch was 2 weeks offshore and 2 weeks at home.

The certification test questions and corresponding correct answers that are pertinent to the accident have been bolded below:

Question: What needs to be inspected before operating Pipe Handler?

    1. **Work area and ensure personnel are clear of area.**

    2. Magnets and load cells to ensure all holding pins are in place.

    3. Hydraulic leaks and rollers on the track.

    4. Electrical cables in drag chain and drag chain.

    5. Check condition of pipe handler and operator's cab.

Question: What needs to be checked before moving pipe handler along the track?

    1. Ensure that gates are down on the track over catwalk.

    2. **Inspect path to ensure no obstructions can restrict the movement of the pipe handler.**

Question: True or False: Personnel can enter work area while the pipe handler is in motion?

False

Question: True or False: Anyone has the right to shut down the pipe handling operation at any time.

True

The Panel was not provided any other training or hazard identification documents associated with the pipe handler and through MMS interviews with rig personnel no one was aware that any additional documents existed. In addition, the manufacturer's Pipe Handler's Operations and Maintenance Manual does not address any training or hazard analysis; only operation and maintenance.

Environmental Conditions

On the day of the accident, meteorological buoy data was unavailable and the rig has since moved location without maintaining the meteorological records. During the MMS interviews it was noted that the rig personnel's statements were consistent to indicate that on the day of the accident it was very hot, bright and sunny. Also, the National Data Buoy Center recorded the temperature at 1030 hours on the day of the accident to be 25.6 degrees Centigrade (78.08 degrees Fahrenheit) from their coastal Grand Isle, Louisiana weather station (GISL1-8761724). This Grand Isle station is located approximately 100 miles northeast of Green Canyon Block 304.

The Specific Pipe Handler Operation

According to the Operator, the specific pipe handler (*see Figure 2*) operation consisted of retrieving the pipe from the catwalk and traversing the pipe to be stacked onto the pipe bay deck. The pipe handler incorporates the spinning and torquing functions of the automated roughneck with the automatic hoisting and racking of disconnected sections of pipe. These functions are integrated via computer controlled sequencing, with the Operator enclosed in an environmentally secure cabin.

Immediately prior to the incident, the Operator placed a joint of drill pipe onto the pipe bay deck. Once the pipe was released, the Operator raised the pipe handler arm up to its full height and proceeded to traverse starboard at a rate of approximately 1.4 miles per hour (118 feet per minute) in preparation to retrieve the next joint.

Figure 2 – Major components of the pipe handler

As the pipe handler traversed itself into position along its trolley to transfer the tubulars to the pipe bay deck, a crush point (*see Figure 3*) developed between the pipe handler's lower travel assembly and one of the pipe handler trolley system's vertical support stanchions. Another angle can be used to demonstrate the crush point area (*see Figure 4*), and the obstructed/unobstructed control cabin view of the Operator to the accident area is noted (*see Figures 5 and 6*).

Figure 3 - Crush point location resulting from the pipe handler's lower travel assembly and vertical support stanchion

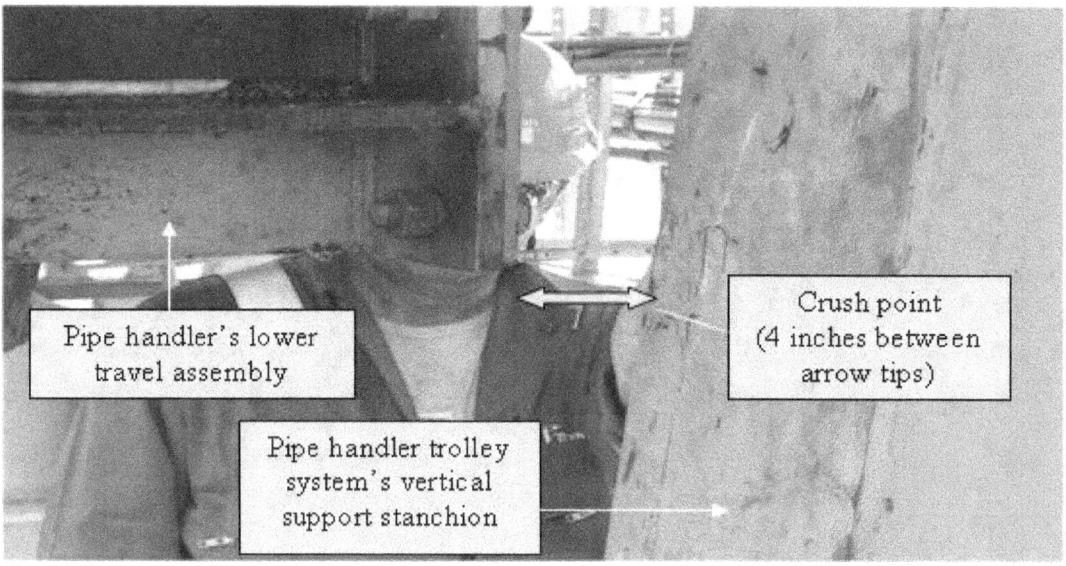

Figure 4 – Another view of the crush point location between the pipe handler's lower travel assembly and vertical support stanchion

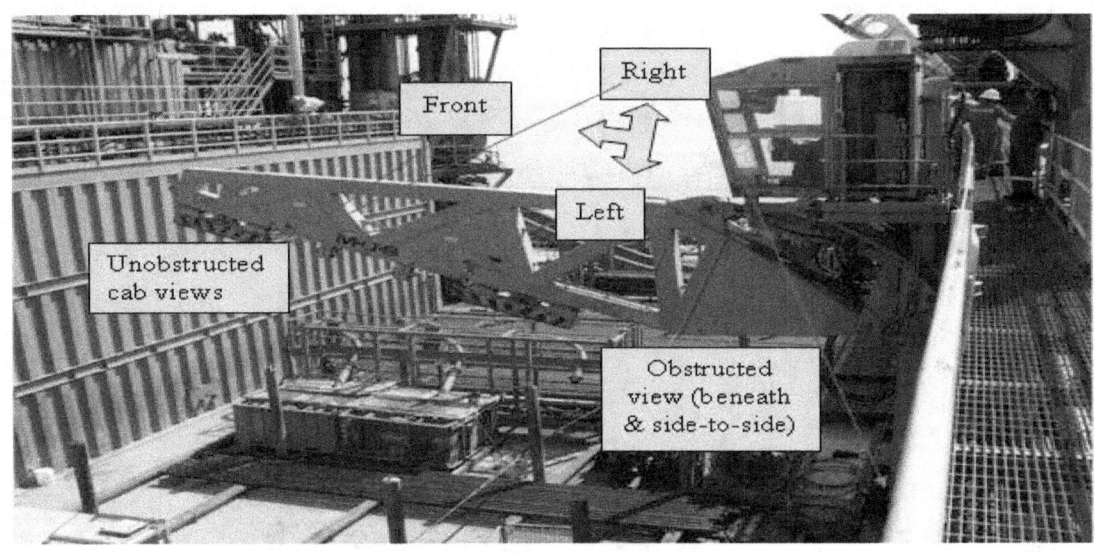

Figure 5 – Unobstructed /obstructed control cabin views of the Spotter and crush point

Figure 6 – Location of accident

At the time of the accident, there were two Painters removing equipment in the next bay from where the Spotter was severely injured and three Roustabouts working with the port pedestal crane back-lading drill collars near the Spotter's position (*see Figures 7 and 8 for position of personnel in both Plan drawing and Photographed View, respectively*).

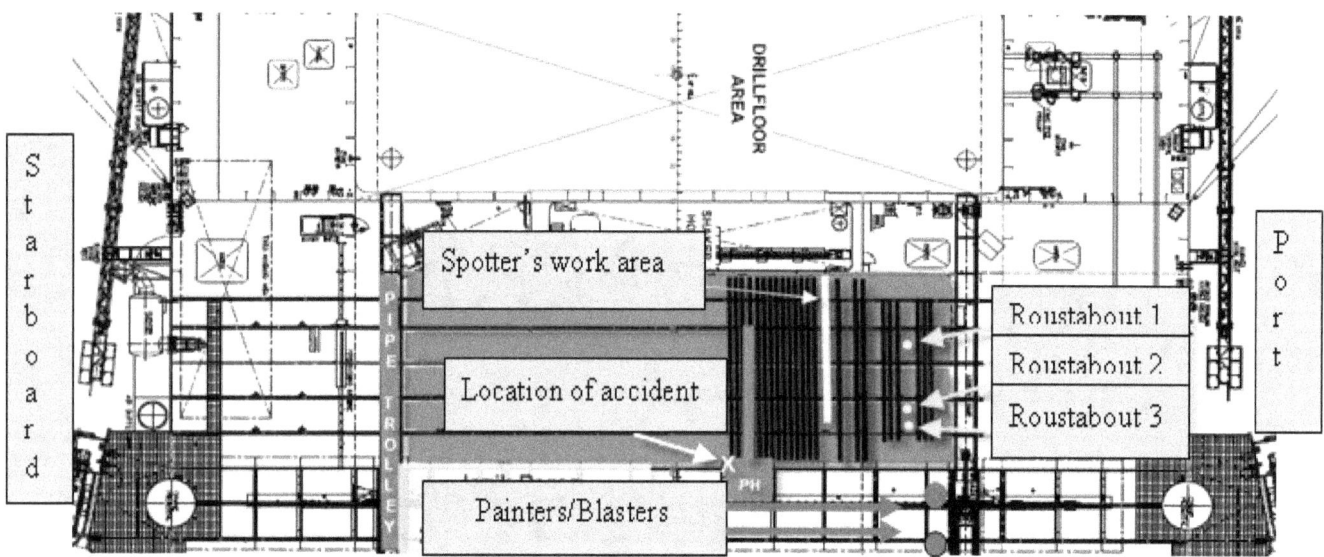

Figure 7 – Personnel positions at time of the accident (Plan)

Figure 8 – Personnel positions at time of the accident (View)

14

Transocean Health and Safety Policies and Procedures Manual (1 August 2009 Revision)

Pertinent excerpts are taken from various sections of the Transocean Health and Safety Policies and Procedures (HSPP) Manual are quoted below by Title, Section and page(s).

General Organization, Roles and Responsibilities - Section 1, Subsection 2
1.9 All Company Personnel (page 4 of 8)

- "Be responsible and accountable for their behavior and for their own safety".

- "Have the obligation and the responsibility not to participate in an unsafe act and also the obligation and responsibility to interrupt any operation to prevent an unsafe act or unsafe condition from causing an incident. Each individual also has the obligation and responsibility to take action to correct any unsafe behavior or condition".

- "Actively support and practice the Company THINK, START and FOCUS processes in order to effectively plan, monitor and improve the HSE aspects of the operation".

General Management of Change (MOC) – Section 1, Subsection 4

The Purpose of the subsection is "to ensure that personnel understand what is required to plan, recognize change and react by interrupting before the change leads to an incident". [Note: The Panel determined that multiple employees were filling new or different roles at the time of the incident. The Panel found that the Transocean Health and Safety Policies and Procedures Manual covering MOC to be confusing and unclear, and were not able to identify any MOC process used by the rig crew prior to the incident.]

4.1 General (pages 1-2 of 11)

"Management of Change is planning, monitoring, recognizing change, interrupting to evaluate the effect of change, and modifying the plan as necessary. The requirements and/or complexity of a task determine the level of management and supervision necessary to ensure appropriate expertise and resources are used to assess the risk, apply controls and develop the plan...Management of Change is used to effectively recognize and manage risks when changes, conditions and inactions in a given situation or unexpected events are experienced. THINK is used by the Company to formulate and communicate the plan. START is used by the Company to monitor the plan and recognize when the plan is no longer suitable. Managing change while performing your task is simply the effective use of THINK and START... FOCUS enhances the execution of THINK and START within the Management of Change process by providing a consistent means to request, track and receive additional expertise (knowledge, experience, skills) and approval from within the organization. If while monitoring a plan, a change is recognized, the task must be interrupted to assess the change and any new risks". [Note: FOCUS refers to Formulate, Organize, Communicate, Undertake and Summarize.]

SPPD Implementing and Monitoring Mechanical Lifting – Section 4, Subsection 5.6
4.8.1 Crane Operators (page 17 of 28)

"Crane Operators must be able to clearly communicate with the handling crew, only one of which may be designated as the Banksman. If the Crane Operator receives instructions or signals from more than one person at a time, the crane operator must interrupt the operation. If the Crane Operator cannot see the Banksman at any time when the load is being moved, he must immediately interrupt the operation and only resume when he has re-established visual contact with the Banksman". [Note: Banksman refers to the Spotter.]

SPPD the THINK Planning Process – Section 4, Subsection 2.1 (pages 21 and 22 of 22)

The Panel located in Figures H1 and H2 of this Subsection what the Think Risk Assessment Prompt Card entails. The Prompt Cards are essentially a Job Safety Analysis that prompts personnel in evaluating operational tasks, hazards and consequences in order to implement control measures to reduce the risk. [Note: According to the Transocean investigation, all supervisors interviewed by the TRIT were unable to demonstrate a clear understanding of the use of Prompt Cards. The Dayshift Deck Pusher had no recollection of having seen the training on Prompt Cards. When the Senior Tool Pusher was interviewed and asked to refer to the HSPP Manual to review the requirement for Prompt Cards use, he could only produce a 2007 HSPP Manual version. According to the Transocean investigation, the TRIT team discovered that although some crew members were aware of the existence of Prompt Cards, they were not generally using them. None of the crew members interviewed were able to demonstrate a complete understanding of the correct use of Prompt Cards. According to the Transocean investigation, the Repsol HSE Representative indicated that he had heard of a few third-party staff using the Prompt Cards on occasion, but he had only heard of them referenced by Transocean management a couple times during pre-tour meetings. He also stated that not all of the 69 Prompt Cards were properly completed over a 4-day period. According to the Transocean investigation, a Transocean rig Performance Monitoring Audit and Assessment carried out in May identified an opportunity for action improvement by the effective use of Prompt Cards, but there is no documentation to demonstrate that the action improvement opportunity was followed.]

SPPD Evaluating the FOCUS Improvement Process – Section 4, Subsection 6.2
1.0   Policy (page 1 of 9)
"The FOCUS Improvement Process must be used to Formulate, Organize, Communicate, Undertake and Summarize corrective and improvement action points to improve Company performance and capture lessons learned".

Repsol Green Canyon Block 304 Drilling Operations Bridging Document (2 April 2009)

As per the Repsol Drilling Operations Bridging Document, the Purpose is to "provide, for different parties involved in the project, a common baseline in terms of policies and procedures, especially for certain environmental and safety related areas. The objectives are:

i)   To reconcile the different standards, practices and/or procedures that the various parties involved in a REPSOL operation may have, in order to obtain consistency.

ii)   To resolve differences, particularly when it comes to implementing certain fundamental procedures where there is room for interpretation and clarification. This will contribute to a permanent state of readiness, especially when prompt reaction and quick decision-making are essential."

3.3.3. Lifting Operations
Section 3.3.3 of the Bridging Document states that the Transocean HQS-HSE-PP-01, Health and Safety – Policies and Procedures Manual, Section 4, Subsection 5.6, 4.8.1

is "in accordance with REPSOL standards and will be used aboard the CAJUN EXPRESS to manage lifting operations". A pertinent excerpt from the Transocean Manual Section 4, Subsection 5.6, 4.8.1, states that the Crane Operator must "be able to clearly communicate with the handling crew, only one of which may be designated as the Banksman. If the Crane Operator receives instructions or signals from more than one person at a time, the Crane Operator must interrupt the operation. If the Crane Operator cannot see the Banksman at any time when the load is being moved, he must immediately interrupt the operation and only resume when he has re-established visual contact with the Banksman".

[Note: During the MMS interviews the Panel confirmed that the Operator and Spotter would keep periodic radio communication as well as visual confirmation, but the Operator only observed the Spotter 30-40% of the time the load was actually being moved from the catwalk to the pipe bay deck.]

Spotter's Previous Performance

Spotter's Performance Appraisal and Development Plan

The Spotter 's last three years of Performance Appraisal and Development Plans received an overall performance review of Fully Acceptable for each of these years. During the period of 1 July 2006 through 31 July 2007, areas for performance improvement included: "To work on his motivation", and "To take more initiative when performing tasks and he needs some supervision". For the period of 1 July 2007 through 1 July 2008, areas for performance improvement included: "Needs expected supervision/just needs to take more initiative in planning for next step of job task", "Does not adapt well to changes without complaining", and "Shows a negative attitude to changes – needs to be more flexible". Lastly, for the period 1 July 2008 through 1 July 2009, one area for improvement was: "Need Supervision". The appraisals do not indicate specifically what type of supervision is needed; i.e., mentoring/teaching supervision, motivating supervision, or disciplinary supervision. The Transocean North American Operations Performance Manager indicated that although Transocean was unable to locate the original signed copies of the Performance Appraisal and

Development Plans, the documents were reviewed and discussed between the Spotter and his Supervisors.

Spotter's Notice of Unsatisfactory Performance

According to Transocean Employee Performance Appraisal and Development Plan, there were two Transocean Notices of Unsatisfactory Performance for the Spotter. A Notice of Unsatisfactory Performance was noted on 2 June 2004. The Notice states in part, "Not using safe work practice at the job site. Sitting on guard rail … (4 feet above deck) while painting. (The deceased) needs to be accountable for his behavior and responsible for his safety. As per HSE Policies and Procedures Manual, Section 1 Subsection 3, 2.2.1." Another Notice of Unsatisfactory Performance was issued on 4 August 2007. That Notice states in part, "(The deceased) failed to follow the Banksman's signals and did not follow the stated TSTP on Pipe Handler operations causing a joint of pipe to fall approximately 10 feet. He acknowledged that he was aware of the hazard as discussed in previous meetings, TSTP, and his pipe handler certification taken 28 July 2007". [Note: Both Notices of Unsatisfactory Performance were signed by the deceased].

Subsequent Data
Post-Accident Events

Without performing an all clear, the Operator traversed the pipe handler approximately 16 feet when he noticed that the Spotter was injured, at which point the Operator immediately pressed the pipe handler's emergency stop. At approximately 1025 hours, the Crane Operator contacted the Medic by phone of a "man down" on the pipe bay deck. The Medic found the injured person lying prone on the deck between the stanchion and a large compactor bag filled with pipe thread protectors. The Medic performed his initial assessment to determine the accident involved severe head trauma. The injured person was determined to be unresponsive and without a pulse. Due to the severe head trauma, no resuscitation efforts were performed, the scene was secured and a Medi-vac helicopter contacted. Medi-vac personnel confirmed the injured person to be deceased upon their arrival and the body was then transported to the West Jefferson Medical Center.

MMS Onsite Investigation and Interviews with Operator and Eyewitness

On 4 September 2009, MMS Houma District Inspectors conducted an onsite investigation of the fatality. Initially, the Inspectors met with the Repsol Senior Company Representative onboard, prior to meeting with the Transocean attorney and TRIT. The MMS Inspectors conducted their accident scene investigation while TRIT conducted their interviews. Numerous photographs were taken by both TRIT and the MMS, and the accident recreated under controlled conditions. One photograph was used to identify the Spotter's suspected rest area with refreshments that included a drink cup on the cable tray, crackers and canned meat on the ledge of the stanchion and partially opened crackers on the deck (*see Figure 9 utilized from the Transocean investigative report).*

The Inspectors met with the Repsol Company Representative and the Transocean Tool Pusher. During this meeting, the MMS Inspectors collected evidence and discussed the accident with the Repsol Senior Company Representative and Transocean Senior Tool Pusher. During this discussion, the MMS Inspectors requested to see a procedure for laying down pipe utilizing the pipe handler. Initially, the MMS Inspectors were told that there was no such procedure, but later in the day the MMS Inspectors were given a Task Specific Think Procedure addressing the use of the pipe handler for transferring pipe to the pipe deck. However, the Task Specific Think Procedure did not mention the location of the Spotter or the potential crush point. Also, the MMS inspectors could find no evidence of past documents describing the pipe handler crush point.

Refreshments: (drink, crackers and canned meat)

Starboard

Port

Pump believed to be used as a seat

Figure 9 – Spotter's suspected rest area with refreshments

Written Statements

Two written statements were recorded on the Transocean Witness Statement Form and copies presented to the MMS on 4 September 2009 during the MMS onsite investigation. Written statements were taken from the Operator and the Painter that witnessed the accident and are quoted verbatim:

Operator:

"During the operation, I was operating the pipe handler and [the deceased] was spotting. During the operation up until the moment of the accident, [the deceased] would duck safely out of the way under the strong-back. When I had traveled up until the accident, I didn't see [the deceased]. I figured he was safely under the strong back waiting for me to travel over out of the way so he could safely do his duty with the pipe handler out of the way. When I traveled over I looked out of the window to see if [the deceased] was going to pop out from under the strong-back. I looked down and saw he was down, so I turned off the pipe handler and got out to see why he was down. That's when I saw how the accident turned out."

Painter/Witness:

"I was cleaning the pressure washer machine when I looked up and saw [the deceased] get hit on the right side of the head by the pipe handler. The pipe handler was moving and hit [the deceased] on the right side of his head. [The deceased] dropped to his knees and then to the floor face down."

Interviews

Other pertinent statements taken during the MMS interviews with the Operator included:

Operator:

- A verbal Think Plan was conducted between the Operator and Spotter prior to the pipe handler operation to include the Spotter's duties and the use of "Stop Work" authority as required. The Operator also stated that it was the rig's policy that a verbal Think Plan was used for two personnel and a Written Think Plan for more than two personnel. [Note: Both the MMS interviews and Transocean-Repsol investigative team notes revealed that the Deck Pusher and Crane Operator believed the Assistant Driller was to be the responsible task supervisor for the Pipe Handler operation. However, the Assistant Driller, the Roustabouts conducting the tasks, and the Offshore Installation Manager for the rig's overall operations, indicated that the Deck Pusher and Crane Operator were the task supervisors.]

- The Operator observed that the trolley path was clear of any obstructions prior to initiating the operation, and the Spotter placed four plastic barriers with red tape at the starboard stairway rig floor, shakers' house entrance and exit, and the catwalk.

- The Spotter's duties were discussed to include setting up the barriers, making sure no personnel were in the area, observing the trolley path for any obstructions, and making sure any pipe did not hit the shaker house.

- It was the Operator's belief that the Operator was always in charge of the pipe handler operation with no other onsite management assistance required.

- The Operator was unaware of the previous disciplinary warnings issued to the Spotter.

- The Operator and Spotter would keep periodic radio communication as well as visual confirmation. The Operator indicated that he observed the Spotter 30-40% of the time the load was actually being moved from the catwalk to the pipe bay deck.

- The Operator indicated that he and the Spotter only worked 12 hour shifts and were beginning to work their third week the day of the accident (which is one week over their normal schedule).

- The Operator indicated that no supervisors visited the work site before or during the task, and both he and the Spotter managed themselves.

23

Painter/Witness

During the MMS interviews with the Painter/Witness, he indicated that the Roustabouts and Painters/Blasters working the pipe bay deck would always remain clear of the pipe handler traversing arm, but there was no specific safety meeting to discuss this.

TRIT Interview Notes and Follow-up MMS Interviews

Fourteen (14) interviews were conducted from 4-6 September 2009 by a team of Transocean and Repsol senior management with pertinent information summarized or quoted verbatim (if it appears in quotes) from the TRIT interview notes and listed below. Personnel's years of experience are also included as it appeared on the TRIT interview notes. MMS interviews were used to confirm the TRIT interview notes, with any additional pertinent information outlined in brackets below the TRIT interview notes listed below.

4 September 2009:

Operator:

The Operator held a verbal discussion of the Spotter's duties with the Spotter at the pipe handling deck to include setting up the barriers, making sure no personnel were in the area, observing the trolley path for any obstructions, and making sure any pipe did not hit the shaker house. The Operator and Spotter worked the pipe handler and performed housekeeping without a break from approximately 0300 hours until they went together to have a meal at approximately 0530 hours. They returned at approximately 0600 hours and continued moving pipe in preparation for the pipe coming from the rig floor at approximately 0730 hours. The Operator stated that he did not feel as though he needed a break because he was in an air conditioned cab. He also indicated that although the Spotter was working in direct sunlight, the Spotter was staying hydrated by getting water from the port crane pedestal water cooler. The Operator mentioned that the Spotter had been ducking back under the pipe handler and the frequency increased as the morning progressed. Although the Operator believed this was unsafe, he did not stop the Spotter because he believed this to be an accepted practice, and was comfortable with the Spotter's experience level since the Spotter had more time on the rig than he did. The Operator stated that the Spotter was "senior to him and had more experience in the task, he did not feel it was his place to question his movements and call a Time Out for Safety". The Operator indicated no supervisors visited the site, and there were no planned or unplanned Time Out for Safety periods taken. The Operator indicated that he placed a joint of drill pipe onto the pipe bay deck, and raised the pipe handler arm to its full height to traverse the pipe handler approximately 16 feet when he noticed the Spotter was injured. The Operator then immediately pressed the emergency stop and medical attention was initiated on the Spotter. During the post-accident TRIT interview, the Operator indicated that he did not always use the radio to ensure an all-clear when the Spotter was not in his direct line of sight. The Operator also stated that he used the radio on some occasions, but did not confirm an all-clear immediately prior to the accident. The Operator indicated that it was unsafe when the Spotter was out of his line of sight, yet he continued to operator the pipe handler when he could only see the Spotter 30-40% of the time. [Note: The aforementioned Operator discussion was summarized by MMS from the Transocean Level 1 Investigation Report completed on 16 September 2009. The TRIT did not provide MMS with a separate Operator interview summary.]

Painter/Witness: 3 weeks aboard the Cajun Express
He also indicated that a Written Think Plan meeting did not include the hazard of moving equipment. The Painter completed cleaning oil and grease from the compressor located in the vicinity of the accident's location and was cleaning the pressure washer machine, but he did not specifically recall seeing the Spotter prior to the event. He noted there were two other paint crew members in the area with one next to him facing away from the pipe deck and the other working across the strong-back. Although the Painter stated he didn't see the actual point of impact since his view was blocked by a beam, he did see the Spotter's head "bashed" after being hit, and signaled the other Roustabouts working in the area. One of the Roustabouts approached him and asked the Painter to step back because of the pipe handler's siren alarm being activated by the Operator. The Painter responded to the TRIT that he did

not recall if his supervisor talked to him about the siren-type alarm meaning to get out of the way [Note: During the MMS interview the Painter indicated that the Roustabouts and Painters/Blasters working on or in the pipe bay deck would always remain clear of the pipe handler traversing arm, but there was no specific safety meeting to discuss this.]

Deck Pusher (DP): 8 years Cajun Express rig experience
The DP attended the morning meeting at 0700 hours, and then made his rounds throughout the rig with the Dispatcher. At one point, he noted the Operator laying down pipe with the Spotter on the pipe bay deck where he believed the Spotter should have been standing. The DP then indicated that the Task Specific Think Plans included moving the pipe with the pedestal cranes for the rig floor and catwalk areas, but did not include the pipe handling operation. The DP also stated that a written procedure requiring a Spotter is needed when Range 3 pipe is being moved. When asked about the pipe handler operation, the DP indicated that the pipe handler operation should have been addressed by the Assistant Driller. He further stated that a Task Specific Think Plan for moving pipe on the pipe deck should be addressed by the Roustabouts, the Crane Operator, or the Lead Hand. When asked how the Crane Operators are trained and mentored he stated, "I look them over", and then stated that he defines a mentor as "an individual taking them around the rig showing them the things they need to do". The DP explained that on-the-job training is performed by the Crane Operator, and the DP expected the Crane Operator to know all the training requirements. When asked how the DP gets involved in the training, the DP stated, "Not a whole lot, I watch them." When asked how he recognizes if someone is ready to be a Crane Operator, the DP stated, "I would see how they work." When asked about the Start program (Prompt Cards), the DP stated, "They (the OIMs) want you to have one card a day", and "They give the cards to the Crane Operator at the pre-tour meeting and he gives them to the Tool Pusher." Later the DP stated, "The OIM told us at pre-tour that they were for use when working alone." When the DP was asked if he looks at them, he replied, "No, only the STOP work authorities." When asked how often the DP performs his deck observations he was noted as replying, "Not often. It would be a good thing but it would not normally be on my mind."

26

When the DP was asked if the majority of the rig personnel believed Prompt Cards was a number's game, he replied, "All think it is." [Note: The DP was terminated from Transocean and MMS was unable to establish contact and conduct an interview because his telephone had been disconnected.]

Acting Deck Foreman (ADF): 3 years Cajun Express rig experience

Although the ADF had 3 years of experience on this rig, he had only been working with this crew since 2 September 2009. The ADF, whose regular duty is a Crane Operator, indicated that he came on at 1130 hours and spent the majority of his day assisting with rig floor crane duties and conducting Written Think Plans on the rig floor with all of the Roustabouts. The crew's main duty was to perform housekeeping on the deck and move the elevators from the port side to the starboard side of the rig floor. When the ADF was asked how he handles risk associated with the Pipe Handler operation, the ADF explained that the crew knew to stand to the aft side of the pipe deck next to the shakers. He also indicated that although it's not included in the Task Specific Think Procedure, it's thoroughly understood by all. The ADF indicated he was very familiar with the Transocean safety protocols and explained that although testing is all well and good, it takes hands-on training (referring to the pipe handler operation). The ADF also stated that the duty of the Spotter was to ensure the pipe did not strike the wind walls or the tensioners. [Note: During MMS interviews, the ADF indicated that there were no procedures in place to prevent entry into the strong-back area. He also stated that Transocean now has a stand-alone Task Specific Think Plan to operate the pipe handler which consists of a "no-go" zone across the strong-back. He also indicated that he never received any information from Transocean management on the Spotter's past employee performance history while the Spotter was under his direct supervision.]

Acting Crane Operator (ACO): 2-1/2 years on the Cajun Express

The ACO, whose regular duty is a Roustabout, indicated he was on the deck by 0530 hours to take a look around and size-up the pipe to be back-loaded with the pedestal crane. He reviewed the Written Think Plan drills with the crew and began the back-loading operation between 0630 and 0700 hours. The ACO stated he did not see the

Spotter near the strong-back area, but that the Spotter was usually wrapping slings on pipe or near the shaker wall area. While the ACO was in the pedestal crane's control cabin, he recalled the Spotter was only in view of the pipe deck area for limited periods of time. The ACO indicated that rig personnel crossing under the strong-back area is the most overlooked hazard, and whenever he operated the pipe handler he always made sure his Spotter was along the shaker wall. The ACO stated he heard and believes it's possible to be surprised by the pipe handler, but he didn't believe to the degree of causing an injury/fatality. He added it is very possible for people to "pop under the strong back." [Note: The ACO was terminated from Transocean and MMS was unable to establish contact and conduct an interview because his telephone had been disconnected.]

Roustabout 1 (Rstb 1): 5 years total experience (previously a Driller on land rigs), but 3rd hitch offshore.

At the time of the accident, Rstb 1 was back-loading the tubulars from the pipe bay deck. He heard the pipe handler coming towards him while the pipe was being lowered to approximately 3 feet off the pipe bay deck. Rstb 1 then turned around to face his task and turned around again because the Painter was "hollering". Rstb 1 stated, "I thought [the Spotter] slipped off the pipe and I hollered on the radio for the Crane Operator to call the Medic. Rstb 1 indicated that the Spotter was not suppose to be under the strong-back when the equipment is moving, but stated that "the strong-back guys walk through all the time." [Note: This is confirmed in the Transocean Pipe Handler Certification test that states "Personnel cannot enter the work area while the pipe handler is in motion".] According to the TRIT notes, he was aware of the Transocean Prompt Cards, carried and used the Prompt Cards every day, yet he didn't regularly see people with them. [Note: During the MMS interviews, Rstb 1 stated that the Offshore Installation Manager told him to stay away from the strong-back. He also indicated that it was sunny, clear and very hot, and they were given periodic breaks for 15-20 minutes at the discretion of their immediate supervisors.]

Repsol Senior Company Representative (RSCR):

The RSCR was the Company Man for this well, and was involved in the Hot Work Permit review/approval process and reviewed the Hot Work Permits and Written Think Plans prior to signing them. Beside his Hot Work Permit responsibilities, RSCR indicated he would be verbally informed by the Offshore Installation Manager when a critical path repair or lock-out was required. The RSCR stated that he felt the Written Think Plans came across to the crews as generic and had a tendency to be more out of necessity. He also indicated that the Written Think Plans lacked emphasis in areas where they were warranted. The RSCR indicated he continuously stressed to personnel that they are in no rush to perform their tasks and that both he and his relief prepare a personal plan of action explaining the objectives from task-to-task. He indicated that these action plans are also emailed to the rig supervisors, printed out and openly shared in the pre-tour meetings. [Note: During the MMS interviews, the RSCR indicated to the Panel that Repsol "failed on the case", (the pipe handler operation). He also indicated that Repsol "leaned" on the Transocean rig supervisors to identify certain risk(s) and stop work. He also indicated that the Task Specific Think Plans were too "generic". Lastly, the RSCR mentioned his concerns about the Spotter and Operator performing jobs they weren't familiar with, but he did not become aware of this until the accident occurred.]

5 September 2009:

Repsol HSE Representative (RHSER):

The RSHER indicated that he looked over general Prompt Cards and recalled seeing them only used once when a Written Think Plan was being prepared. He understood the Prompt Cards should be used when preparing for all jobs, but he hadn't personally used them. He indicated that he had heard of a few third-party staff using them on occasion, but only heard of them referenced by management a couple times during pre-tour meetings. He stated that the Written Think Plans were a good process because of the continuous improvement value it added to the program, but added that the process is looked upon/carried out by crews as just "a paperwork exercise." He stated that the push or encouragement typically comes in the form of a threatening approach instead of the approach that it should be used to conduct safer

29

operations. He then stated, "You must do it or you lose your job approach" and indicated that this is the feedback he received from the rig hands during informal conversations. The RHSER then stated that he would commonly find the Deck Pusher on the deck. However, the RHSER believed that the Deck Pushers and Crane Operators are not the best leaders, because although they are proficient with the equipment operations, "the trickle down effects tends to impact their interaction with their crew." He also stated that although deck supervision has good intentions, the crew "act or perform their duties out of fear of losing their job." He cited that not all of the 69 Prompt Cards he reviewed over a 4-day period were properly completed. [Note: During the MMS interviews, the RHSER indicated that rig supervisors on the job should have exercised their supervision over the pipe handler Operator. The RHSER also stated that he was "ignorant" to the hazards of the pipe handler operation, nor was he familiar with the Spotter's past performance history. He also indicated that he participated in the various pre-job and tour safety meetings, but not the pipe handler operation pre-job meeting.]

Offshore Installation Manager (OIM): 34 years total experience, 25 years with Transocean and 3 years on the Cajun Express.

The OIM indicated that the supervisors are involved in every Written Think Plan, but some do more than others by mentoring; yet mentoring is only as good as the quality of the supervisor. [Note: During the MMS interviews it was determined that the OIM did not make it outside to oversee operations prior to the incident occurring. He informed the Panel that the Crane Operator and the Deck Pusher were in charge of the pipe handling operations. The Deck Pusher was encouraged by the OIM to be more involved in deck operations, since the OIM had noticed the lack of the Deck Pusher's involvement in the pipe handler operation prior to the accident. The OIM was aware that the Operator and Spotter did not perform a Task Specific Think Plan for the pipe handler operation since this was only a two-person operation. The OIM also noted that he didn't believe there was a requirement to get an all clear before traversing the pipe handler. The OIM knew the Spotter had past performance issues, but was performing well at his present duties. The OIM also stated that it's mandatory that new personnel participate in both verbal and written Think Plans and must sign the written Think Plans.]

Acting Tool Pusher (ATP): 19 years total experience with 9 years on the Cajun Express

The ATP indicated that it was a short change crew during the day of the accident so there was no pre-tour meeting. He indicated that he went straight to the deck to be in charge of the rig floor cementing job. The ATP indicated that the Spotter (the deceased) "struggled" while working as a Seaman, had "issues" as a Roustabout, but seemed to find his "niche" on the drill floor. He also stated that the Spotter was active in performing risk assessments. [Note: During the MMS interviews the ATP stated that the Spotter was normally under his direct supervision, but the ATP was never informed of the Spotter's past performance history by Transocean management. He also stated that the two onboard Repsol representatives would walk the deck at least once a tour. Lastly, he stated that the Spotter was aware of general high risk areas, and specifically the strong-back area's high risk potential because of the moving pipe handler. However, the MMS could not locate any evidence that anyone was aware of the crush/pinch points of the pipe handler operation prior to the accident.]

Roustabout 3 (Rstb 3): 6 years offshore experience with approximately 1 year on the Cajun Express

Rstb 3 stated that the strong-back area was sometimes used for shaded coverage, and that people did not take seriously the moving hazard of the pipe handler. [The hazard is identified in the Transocean Pipe Handler Certification test and states that "Personnel cannot enter the work area while the pipe handler is in motion".] Rstb 3 also indicated that he had seen personnel standing under the strong-back watching the pipe handler pass very close to them. He noted that the sling rack is usually positioned more aft towards the shaker wall and spotting the pipe handler seemed hectic since it was difficult getting the slings on and out of the way prior to the pipe handler coming rack around. He also remembered observing the Spotter having difficulty with some clamps earlier during the tour, and believed that two people were recently terminated as a result of an incident involving the pipe handler. [Note: During the MMS interviews Rstb 3 indicated that even though they were warned about the strong-back area during certification testing/training, the strong-back area was often used as shade due to the high ambient temperature. He also indicated that the area was easily accessible and rig personnel took shortcuts through the area to get between bays. Rstb 3 indicated that he often saw the Spotter in the strong-back area during the pipe handler operation. He indicated that he believed the accident might have been prevented if additional supervision had been implemented to oversee the pipe handler operation.]

Conclusions

The Accident

It is the conclusion of the Panel that on 3 September 2009 during pipe handler operations, crush points existed between the pipe handler's lower travel assembly and pipe handler trolley system's vertical support stanchions. At 1025 hours, the Operator proceeded to traverse the pipe handler on its trolley system approximately sixteen feet from the mid-ship bay back to the starboard catwalk in preparation to pick-up the next joint. At this time the head of the Spotter was caught in the crush point resulting in a fatal head injury. Based on the Panel's investigation and witness testimony, it is concluded that the Spotter was sitting and/or leaned forward toward the pipe bay deck when the pipe handler struck the Spotter's head from the right side. The Spotter was attended to by the onsite Medic who found no signs of life and was later pronounced deceased by the attending Medi-vac personnel.

Cause

The Operator failed to confirm an "all clear" or a "Time Out for Safety" (Stop Work authority) when the Spotter was out-of-sight:

The two pipe handler paths that must be "clear" during the traversing operation consisted of the path beneath the trolley system and the path beneath the pipe handler arm on the pipe bay deck. However, the Transocean pipe handler certification test only specifies that the "path" needs to be inspected to ensure no obstructions can restrict the movement of the pipe handler. Although the Operator did verify through visual observation that the trolley path was clear of obstructions prior to initiating operations and the pipe bay deck was clear during the operations, he had to rely on the Spotter for confirming that the trolley path remained clear of personnel during the operation. The Operator, therefore, through visual observations did comply with the test question to "make sure personnel are clear of work area" if the work area is defined as the pipe bay deck. The Operator stated during the MMS interview that the pipe bay deck personnel (three Roustabouts and two Painters/Blasters) were always working in the bay away from the traversing arm of the pipe handler. However, the Operator did not ensure that the Spotter was clear of the path beneath the trolley system.

Section 4, Subsection 5.6 for Mechanical Lifting of the Transocean HSPP Manual, states in part under 4.8.1 that Crane Operators "must be able to clearly communicate with the handling crew, only one of which may be designated as the Banksman. If the Crane Operator cannot see the Banksman at any time when the load is being moved, he must immediately interrupt the operation and only resume when he has re-established visual contact with the Banksman". [Note: The Banksman in this policy refers to the Spotter.] Although the Operator could only see the Spotter 30-40% of the time the pipe handler traversed the pipe from the catwalk to the pipe bay deck, the Operator proceeded without calling a Time Out for Safety. It was also discovered by the Panel that the Operator was not aware of previous disciplinary warnings issued to the Spotter.

A portion of Section 1, Subsection 2 for General Organization, Roles and Responsibilities of the Transocean HSPP Manual, states under 1.9 that all company personnel, "Visibly conduct themselves in line with core values, be responsible and accountable for their behavior and their own safety, have the obligation and responsibility not to participate in an unsafe act and the obligation and responsibility to interrupt any operation to prevent an unsafe act or unsafe condition from causing an accident." Although the Spotter exposed himself to the trolley path hazard created by the pipe handler, the Operator did not stop the Spotter from committing this hazardous action. Both the Operator and Spotter were aware of the Transocean Pipe Handler Certification Test question that stated, "Personnel cannot enter the work area while the pipe handler is in motion".

Therefore, the Operator's failure to confirm an "all clear" with the Spotter and not exercising his Stop Work authority when the Spotter was out of the Operator's line-of-sight during the pipe handler operation is concluded to be a cause of the accident.

Contributing Causes

Transocean management failed in providing a more formalized training program to include the hazards associated with the operation of the pipe handler:

The Operator training consisted mainly of on-the-job training with little no class room/textbook training. The Transocean pipe handler certification test is comprised of sixteen fill-in the blank, multiple choice, and true-or-false questions. The test is the same as the study guide, with the exception of the certification test not including the study guide answers. Therefore, memorization of the study guide is all that is required to pass the pipe handler certification test. The last step of the Transocean certification process is observing a qualified Operator for several hitches prior to beginning the hands-on operation of the pipe handler while being observed by the qualified Operator. In addition, the Panel could not locate through document searches or MMS interviews that a more formalized pipe handler training program that incorporates hazard analysis document(s) exists. This creates the potential for unknowing safe actions by the Operator and Spotter since the pipe handler operational risk are not being reduced to as low as reasonably practicable.

Therefore, Transocean management's failure in providing a more formalized pipe handler training program to include the hazards associated with the pipe handler is concluded to be a contributing cause of the accident.

Transocean line management failed to identify the specific pipe handler operational tasks, hazards and respective mitigations in order to develop and implement guidelines for personnel working around the strong-back area:

The MMS interviews determined that the rig personnel's major concern was being hit by the traversing load during the pipe handler operation. However, the crush points that always existed between the traversing pipe handler lower travel assembly and the trolley system's vertical support stanchions had not been identified prior to the accident. The crush point was not identified in the Transocean's investigation report of the Cajun Express pipe handler's falling pipe incident conducted three months prior to this accident. In addition, the crush point was not mentioned in the MOS LTD Operations/Maintenance Manual dated 6 October 2000, manufactured for the Southeast Drilling Company (SEDCO) rigs.

Although temporary "No Entry" handrails had been placed at the starboard rig floor stairway, the exit and entrance of the shaker house, and the catwalk, the area was easily accessible by ducking under the pipe handler trolley system. There were no effective barriers (signage, red zones, tiger striping, temporary barrier tape, handrails, etc.) preventing those working in the area from entering the pipe handler trolley path and the existing crush point. There is also a telephone located near the pipe handler travel path indicating that this area is considered "safe".

35

Based on the TRIT interview notes and the additional MMS interviews, the Panel determined that personnel developed a high risk tolerance for working around and under the strong-back area of the trolley system. According to the TRIT interview notes, Roustabout 1 indicated that the Spotter was not supposed to be under the strong-back when the equipment is moving, but stated that "rig personnel walk through all the time." Roustabout 3 indicated that the strong-back area had been used by personnel for shade and in the past had also seen personnel standing under the strong-back watching the pipe handler pass very close to them. The Acting Crane Operator stated that the strong-back area is the most overlooked hazard. The Acting Crane Operator also stated that he has heard and believes it's possible to be surprised by the pipe handler, but he didn't believe to the degree of causing an injury/fatality. He added it is very possible for people to just "pop-up under the strong-back" beneath the trolley. In addition, the Panel investigation could find no evidence that a specific strong-back policy or guideline existed, nor that supervisors requested or required the crew to cease the practice of entering the strong-back area during pipe handler operations.

Four pre-job safety meetings were conducted by the respective pipe handling crew supervisors and signed by all crew members, utilizing Transocean Written Think Plans, Task Specific Think Plans and corresponding Think Process Checklists for simultaneous pedestal crane operations, but none of these safety meetings and respective documents discussed any of the steps required for the specific pipe handler operation. In addition, according to the TRIT interview notes and MMS interviews, the Repsol Senior Company Representative indicated that he felt the Written Think Plans came across to the crews as "generic, had a tendency to be more out of necessity and lacked emphasis in areas where they were warranted. The Repsol HSE Representative also indicated that the Written Think Plans were looked upon/carried out by crews as just "a paperwork exercise", and the request for using Written Think Plans typically came in the form of a threatening approach. A specific pipe handler Written Think Plan could have addressed areas for planning, inspecting, identifying, communicating and controlling the pipe handling tasks and hazards associated with the pipe handler operation. A generic Task Specific Think Plan that was given to the MMS inspectors later in the day was not used for the pipe handler operation, nor did it identify a crush point. A specific pipe handler Think Process Checklist could have been helpful in identifying the following: 1) the use of effective barriers for potentially hazardous areas, 2) adjacent areas that could be struck by equipment or the moving load, 3) pinch or crush points between objects, 4) the use of personnel who are familiar with the pipe handler operation, 5) clearly defined roles and responsibilities for all pipe handler personnel (including supervision oversight), 6) management of change policy requirements, 7) isolation controls and 8) a detailed pipe handler procedure.

No Prompt Cards were utilized for the pipe handler operation, and for the Prompt Cards that were used the TRIT interview notes identified that the crew members were not able to demonstrate a complete understanding of the correct Prompt Card use. The Repsol HSE Representative indicated that the Prompt Cards being used were being completed improperly. Therefore, the Prompt Cards were not being utilized effectively as a job safety analysis tool with the intent to prompt rig personnel in evaluating operational tasks, hazards and consequences. The use of a specific pipe handler Prompt Card could assist in implementing control measures to reduce the risk.

Therefore, Transocean line management's failure to identify the specific pipe handler operational tasks, hazards and respective mitigations in order to develop and implement strong-back guidelines is concluded to be a contributing cause of the accident.

Transocean's line management failed to exercise the required additional onsite supervision to both the Operator and Spotter during the pipe handler operation:

Based on the MMS interviews, the OIM indicated that the Deck Pusher and Crane Operator were in charge of the pipe handler operation. The Deck Pusher stated he did not go to the worksite at any time during the pipe handler operation, but indicated that from another deck level he noted that the Spotter was in the correct Spotter position. The Acting Crane Operator was solely involved in back-loading the tubulars to the cargo vessel utilizing the pedestal crane, and therefore did not supervise the pipe handler operation. The Operator also indicated that no additional rig supervisor visited the worksite between 0600 hours and the time of the accident at 1025 hours.

In addition, the Spotter had under-performed previous deck duties, received previous disciplinary warnings, and was identified to require an expected amount of supervision. The Spotter received Notices of Unsatisfactory Performance in regards to sitting on the guard rail while painting (2 June 2004) and while operating the pipe handler failed to follow the Banksman signals resulting in a joint of pipe falling approximately 10 feet (4 August 2007). The pipe handler operational risk could have been reduced to as low as reasonable practicable if the proper additional onsite supervision had been provided. The Panel believes that if this additional Crane Operator and Deck Pusher oversight had been provided for the pipe handing operation, there was a greater potential for the Transocean written safety documents to be provided for all personnel involved in this operation. These documents could have addressed the pipe handler operational tasks, hazards and respective mitigations.

The Spotter's last three years of Performance Appraisal and Development Plans received an overall performance review of Fully Acceptable for each of these years. However, all three performance reviews state that the Spotter required supervision. The appraisals do not indicate specifically what type of supervision is needed; i.e., mentoring/teaching supervision, motivating supervision, or disciplinary supervision. However, the Spotter's previous 2007 Notice of Unsatisfactory Performance would indicate that he was in need of some form of additional supervisory oversight. In addition, based on the MMS interviews the OIM stated that he knew the Spotter had past performance history issues.

Therefore, Transocean line management's failure to exercise the required supervisory oversight of the Crane Operator and Deck Pusher for the pipe handler operation is concluded to be a contributing cause of the accident.

Transocean's line management failed to properly implement their Management of Change policy:

The regular Toolpusher, Deck Foreman and Assistant Crane Operator were all on personal leave, and a Roustabout had passed away on his time off. This created a need to change personnel positions and bring personnel from another crew. At one point during the pipe handler operation, a Roustabout with a Class B Operator's certification was designated the Acting Crane Operator and task supervisor to manage multiple tasks with a newly created crew. Another Roustabout with less than twelve days industry experience, and only nine days Cajun Express experience, was also allowed to act as a relief Spotter, with the Floorhand Roustabout (deceased) acting in the pipe handler Spotter capacity. This need for a short change crew resulted in implementing the Transocean Management of Change policy. However, there was no pre-tour rig safety meeting held on the rig for the short change shift crew involved in the accident. Accepted practice on the rig was not to hold a pre-tour meeting during the short change crew, despite the fact that pre-tour meetings are required as part of the regular crew change process. A pre-tour meeting for the short change crew shifts could be beneficial in addressing the safety aspects of any operation being conducted by personnel filling new roles and/or not working on their normal duties.

The Transocean Management of Change policy in place at time of the accident required all personnel involved in the incident to understand what is required to plan (recognize change and react by interrupting before the change leads to an incident) the task at hand. However, the Panel investigation did not reveal any form of a procedure or other information indicating the Transocean Management of Change policy was followed by those involved in the incident.

In addition, the Panel found the Transocean Management of Change policy to be confusing for the following reasons: 1) the policy is eleven pages, 2) it utilizes all Transocean safety plans, 3) one of three approaches must be selected for assessing a change and 4) the intricate nature of the policy hinders the ability to recognize, assess, and interpret any new hazards associated with the change.

Therefore, Transocean line management's failure to properly implement the confusing Management of Change policy with the short change crew is concluded to be a contributing cause of the accident.

Possible Contributing Cause

The work area involved a hot working environment in direct sunlight:

The MMS interviews with the Operator indicated that he was not that concerned about the heat secondary to working in the pipe handler air-conditioned cab, and he believed the Spotter was getting regular drinks from the crane pedestal area while being shaded from the sun beneath the pipe handler trolley area. He stated that the Spotter was working in direct sunlight on a hot day and repeatedly moved in and out of the shaded trolley area after the sun came up. No breaks were taken during the 4-1/2 hour period from 0600 hours until the time of the accident at 1025 hours. The Acting Crane Operator had one person identified to relieve the Operator and/or Spotter but assigned this individual to another task. Lastly, it would appear from the Transocean photograph in Figure 9 that the Spotter utilized the Wilden pump as a shaded rest area with refreshments under the pipe handler trolley, thereby requiring his need to periodically duck in and out of sight from the Operator.

Although the Panel was unable to acquire any meteorological data for the location during the accident day, the Panel utilized the consistent statements derived from the MMS interviews that indicated the accident day was very sunny and hot. In addition, the National Data Buoy Center recorded the temperature at 1030 hours on the day of the accident to be 25.6 degrees Centigrade (78.08 degrees Fahrenheit) from their coastal Grand Isle, Louisiana weather station (GISL1-8761724). This station is located approximately 100 miles northeast of Green Canyon Block 304.

The hot work environment is considered to be a possible contributing cause of the accident because the Spotter repeatedly moved into the shaded area of the trolley system across the pipe handler's traversing path when he was not assisting the Operator.

Recommendations

The investigative Panel recommends that the MMS should issue a Safety Alert to industry regarding this accident. The Safety Alert should briefly describe the accident and identify all causes with the following recommendations made to Lessees, Operators and their contractors for any type of overhead trolley beam mounted crane (trolley crane) operation, including but not limited to a pipe handler:

- The trolley crane operations should be inspected with the intent to identify all potential hazards (including pinch/crush points) with their respective mitigations, and communicate these findings with all necessary personnel.

- The trolley crane's path should be kept clear and not used for storage. Telephones, intercoms or stored items located under the trolley crane should be removed and relocated to a safer area.

- Safety barriers (signage, red zones, tiger striping, temporary barrier tape, handrails, etc.) should be installed and maintained to prevent access to the trolley crane's traversing path.

- In areas where the view is obstructed to the trolley crane Operator, consideration should be given to the feasibility of installing cameras or mirrors in areas where the Operator's view is obstructed.

- Consider the feasibility of re-engineering the trolley crane to possibly eliminate any additional Spotter involvement.

- The use of a Stop Work authority program should be reviewed with personnel, while focusing on the importance of the individual's responsibilities to exercise Stop Work authority as necessary.

- Pre-tour meetings should be held prior to all tours, including short change crews. The short change crew involves multiple employees filling new roles and/or not working on their normal crew shift during the time of the accident.

- The installation's Management of Change policy should be reviewed for clarity and to ensure that the policy recognizes and manages changes, conditions and inactions in a given situation or unexpected events.

- A formalized trolley crane training program should be utilized to ensure that the program covers not only the proper operation of the equipment, but also includes the limitations, capabilities and potential hazards. If the training includes hands-on training, the verification/certification should be done by senior facility management.